Gpjc
6-12

W9-DIL-396

SUPER TRIVIA COLLECTION

THIS BOOK MIGHT BITE

BY MEGAN COOLEY PETERSON

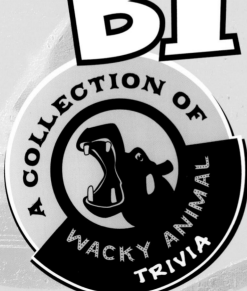

A COLLECTION OF WACKY ANIMAL TRIVIA

Content Consultant:
Dwight Lawson, PhD
Deputy Director
Zoo Atlanta
Atlanta, Georgia

CAPSTONE PRESS
a capstone imprint

Edge Books are published by Capstone Press,
1710 Roe Crest Drive, North Mankato, Minnesota 56003.
www.capstonepub.com

Books published by Capstone Press are manufactured with paper
containing at least 10 percent post-consumer waste.

Library of Congress Cataloging-in-Publication Data
Peterson, Megan Cooley.
    This book might bite : a collection of wacky animal trivia / by Megan Cooley Peterson.
    p. cm. — (Edge. Super trivia collection)
    Includes bibliographical references and index.
    Summary: "Includes interesting facts about various animals enhanced by photos,
illustrations, and clever dialogue bubbles"—Provided by publisher.
    ISBN 978-1-4296-7655-7 (library binding)
    1. Animals—Miscellanea—Juvenile literature. I. Title. II. Series.
QL49.P396 2012
590—dc23   2011034674

Editorial Credits
Mandy Robbins, editor; Alison Thiele, designer; Svetlana Zhurkin, media specialist;
    Laura Manthe, production specialist

Photo Credits
Alamy: blickwinkel, 13 (bottom), 15 (top), Poelzer Wolfgang, 27 (bottom); Corbis: National
Geographic Society/Mauricio Handler, 28 (top), Visuals Unlimited/Alex Wild, 8 (middle),
Visuals Unlimited/Ken Catania, 17 (top); Dreamstime: Mgkuijpers, 20 (right); Getty Images:
Max Gibbs, 11, Minden Pictures/Konrad Woth, 13 (top); iStockphoto: Chase Swift, 18 (top);
National Geographic Stock: Minden Pictures/Mark Moffett, 27 (top); Nova Development
Corporation, 3, 10 (middle), 12 (left), 14 (bottom), 17 (bottom), 18 (bottom), 19 (middle and
bottom), 20 (left), 25 (middle and bottom), 26 (top), 28 (bottom), 29 (top); Photo Researchers:
Valerie Giles, 25 (top); Photodisc, 21 (bottom right); SeaPics: David Wrobel, 16, J. J. Perez
Torres, 5 (top); Shutterstock: Alan Jeffery, 15 (bottom), Arnoud Quanjer, 23, Atovot, 7
(bottom), Cameramannz, 19 (top), Claudiu Mihai Badea, 10 (top), Denis Barbulat, 6–7
(top), Dennis Donohue, 29 (middle), Dr. Morley Read, 4–5 (bottom), Edwin Verin, 21 (top),
Fernando Cortes (background), cover and throughout, Hugh Lansdown, 14 (top), kurt_G,
cover (bottom middle), 26 (middle), LilKar, 10 (bottom), Mariette Budel, 9, Michael Lynch,
cover (bottom right), 6, mountainpix, 22 (top), Nathalie Speliers Ufermann, cover (top), back
cover, 24, Nip, 8 (top), Photofish, 18 (middle), Sari ONeal, 22 (bottom), Susan Flashman, 12
(right), YorkBerlin, 21 (bottom left)

**The author dedicates this book to Jessica Benschoter, who didn't let a little thing like being
allergic to animals stop her from becoming a zookeeper.**

Printed in the United States of America in Stevens Point, Wisconsin.
102011   006404WZS12

TABLE OF CONTENTS

STRANGE BUT TRUE

A hairy-looking frog. A bug that hears with its knees. A snail that blows bubbles. These animals aren't creatures from a horror movie. They're all real.

Some animal bodies, behaviors, and homes might seem odd to us. But animals have adapted to live in their habitats. They have unique ways of finding food and staying safe. Animals keep what works and change what doesn't.

The animals featured in this book act and look so strange, they might seem unbelievable. But when it comes to animals, sometimes truth is stranger than fiction! So flip the page, and get ready to meet some real freaks of nature.

adapt—to change in order to survive; a change in an animal or plant is called an adaptation

Chapter 1
WHAT'S FOR LUNCH?

Animals whip up all sorts of meals. But their idea of a tasty meal is probably different than yours. You might not want to eat after reading about some strange animal cuisine.

You wouldn't want to invite a vampire bat to lunch. Not only do vampire bats drink animal blood, they pee while they eat! These bats lap up half their body weight in blood each night. Peeing helps them lose weight so they can fly away.

Aardvarks gobble up to 50,000 termites and ants in a single night.

Rabbits enjoy their food so much they eat it twice. They have two kinds of droppings—hard, brown feces and soft balls filled with important nutrients. The soft droppings are coated with mucus so they aren't digested. Rabbits eat them to get nutrients from plants that are hard to digest.

Meat cookie, anyone? Cookiecutter sharks feast on tuna, swordfish, whales, and dolphins. But they don't just take a bite and swim away. These sharks sink sharp teeth into their victims and spin in a circle. Then they suck out a "cookie" of flesh.

Some honeypot ants become so fat with stored honeydew they can no longer walk. Instead they hang upside down inside the nest to serve as living food containers. Other ants eat their vomit.

Jackals don't waste their food. They eat dead animal flesh and feed their young by vomiting. If the young can't finish their food, the adults eat their own puke.

Cows eat a high-fiber diet of grass, which causes them to burp and fart almost constantly. In the United States, cows release 6 million tons (5.4 million metric tons) of methane gas each year.

Baby koalas eat their mothers' soupy poop. The special poop is called pap. It is filled with important microorganisms. The microorganisms prepare the young koalas' digestive systems for a diet of toxin-filled eucalyptus leaves.

methane—a colorless, odorless gas that burns easily
microorganism—a living thing too small to be seen without a microscope
toxin—a poisonous substance produced by a living thing

Humpback whales can reach lengths of more than 60 feet (18 meters). They have appetites as big as their bodies. These whales often hunt in groups. They surround schools of fish with air bubbles. The bubbles trap the fish like a net. The whales then swim through the net to feast on the fish buffet.

The tiger shark didn't earn the nickname "wastebasket of the sea" for nothing. License plates, tires, fast-food wrappers, and even a set of antlers have been found inside tiger sharks' stomachs.

Honey might be tasty, but the way honey bees make it is anything but sweet. First, worker bees store nectar in their honey stomachs, which break down the nectar's sugars. Back at the hive, they vomit the nectar. The water evaporates, and the bee barf becomes honey.

nectar—a sweet liquid that honey bees gather from flowers

evaporate—the action of a liquid changing into a gas; heat causes water to evaporate

Candiru catfish get attached to their food. These tiny fish live in the Amazon River. Candiru catfish swim into the gills of larger fish and latch on with hooks located on their heads. Then they suck up blood for 30 seconds to three minutes.

Watch Where You Pee

Fish gills aren't the only places candiru catfish swim into. In 1997 a man swimming in the Amazon River decided to pee in it. A few days later, doctors found a dead candiru catfish lodged in his urethra. Scientists believe the candiru may have confused the man's urine with chemicals that larger fish leave behind. The fish then followed the urine to its source. Although the candiru rarely latches on to humans, you probably wouldn't want to pee in the Amazon River!

Chapter 2

HOME SWEET HOME

Animals, like people, need places to live. Some of these homes are just plain weird. Check out some of the oddest places animals call home.

African termites build nests that look like skyscrapers. They build these nests out of clay and spit. A single nest can rise more than 25 feet (7.6 m) above the ground. That's taller than the average adult male giraffe!

We should have built an elevator.

The world's largest badger burrow ever found contained 2,883 feet (879 m) of underground tunnels. The burrow had 50 rooms and 178 entrances.

The edible-nest swiftlets of Asia build their nests almost entirely out of spit. The male birds attach spit strings to rock walls, and the spit hardens. What's more surprising? Some people in Asia use the nests to make bird's nest soup.

Burying beetles build disgusting homes for their young. They bury dead animals, such as birds and mice. The females lay their eggs near the bodies. When the young hatch, they have a "fresh" supply of rotting meat to feast on.

Not all ants call underground nests home. Weaver ants build nests out of leaves and silk. First, worker ants pull two leaves together. Others glue them together using silk from *larvae*. They move the larvae back and forth like tiny sewing machines.

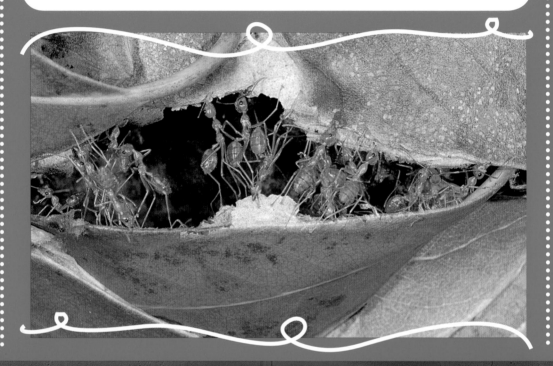

Have you ever blown a spit bubble? Now imagine living on it! Violet sea snails live in the ocean but can't swim. They build rafts out of mucus bubbles that float on the water's surface. The snails hang upside down from the bubbles their entire lives. If the rafts break, the snails drown.

larva—an insect at the stage after an egg; more than one larva are larvae

Old houses and dark basements aren't the only places creepy, crawly spiders call home. European water spiders spend most of their lives in water but breathe air. These spiders spin bell-shaped silk nests underwater. Then they fill the nests with air bubbles.

The world's largest beaver dam was discovered in Canada in 2007. It was about 2,800 feet (850 m) long. That's as long as eight football fields!

Chapter 3
AMAZING BODIES

Some animals might look like they're dressed up in Halloween costumes. But their odd-looking bodies help them find food, stay safe, and fight off enemies. Learn about some of nature's most amazing animal bodies.

Can you imagine large, glowing green eyes staring out at you from inside a see-through head? The Pacific barreleye fish has tube-shaped eyes that are visible through its head. Tubular eyes collect more light in deep waters. A see-through head protects the fish's eyes from the stings of deep-sea jelly fish.

The star-nosed mole has 22 pink tentacles on its nose. It uses them to identify food by touch. Star-nosed moles can find, identify, and eat an insect in less than one second.

The blue whale is the world's largest animal. Its heart weighs as much as a small car. Its tongue is the size of an adult elephant.

The next time you hear someone say he's "sweating like a pig," share this fact—pigs don't sweat! Because they don't have sweat glands, pigs relax in mud to keep cool.

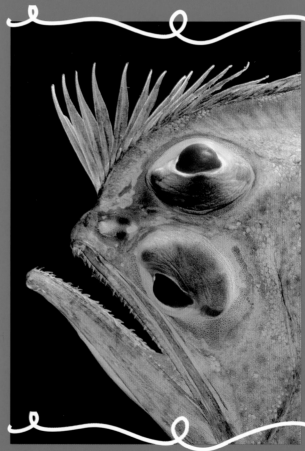

To blend in with the ocean floor, flatfish spend their entire adult lives lying on their sides. They have eyes on only one side of their heads. At birth, they look like regular fish until one eye moves to the opposite side of the head.

A cricket's ears are located in each of its front legs below the knees.

The tuatara is a reptile with a third eye on top of its head. The eye has a lens and a retina. It's connected to the brain by a nerve. Although scales cover the eye, it is sensitive to light and may help the tuatara control body temperature. Other reptiles have less-developed third eyes.

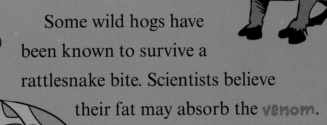

Some wild hogs have been known to survive a rattlesnake bite. Scientists believe their fat may absorb the venom.

venom—a poisonous liquid produced by some animals

If rats and mice give you the creeps, you wouldn't want to meet a capybara. The capybara is the world's largest rodent. Found in Central and South America, it can weigh more than 100 pounds (45 kilograms).

The skin of a wild golden poison dart frog can contain enough venom to kill 20,000 mice or 10 adult humans. Just holding one of these deadly frogs may kill you.

An African elephant's trunk contains about 100,000 muscles. The human body has between 650 and 850 muscles. Elephants use their trunks to breathe, eat, drink, and pick up objects.

Tarsiers are small animals with huge eyes. In fact, each eye is as big as its brain! Tarsiers are *nocturnal*, and large eyes help them see well at night. Since they can't move their eyes, tarsiers rotate their heads like owls.

Some scientists believe Tyrannosaurus rex's closest living relative may be the chicken. They claim that proteins found in a 68-million-year-old T-rex bone closely match those found in chickens.

Grandpa?

nocturnal—active at night and resting during the day

People once believed that hippopotamuses sweated blood. But the oily, red substance that oozes from their skin is really a built-in sunscreen.

Delicious!

Female butterflies test out food for their young. They taste plants with their feet to make sure they're safe for caterpillars to feed on.

A polar bear's fur is clear, which allows sunlight to pass through it. Light bouncing off the fur makes it look white. Black skin under the fur absorbs the sun's warmth.

Male African hairy frogs grow long, hairlike strands of skin from their bodies during mating season. The "hairs" help the frogs breathe through their skin as they sit on eggs underwater.

Scorpions glow under ultraviolet lights. Proteins in their **exoskeleton** make them **fluorescent**. Scientists aren't sure why they glow.

One Tough Bug

Scorpions are able to survive harsh conditions. Their bodies slow the process of changing food into energy. They can live for a year after eating only one insect. One scientist even froze scorpions. The next day, the scorpions thawed in the sun and walked away.

OUTRAGEOUS WACKY ANIMAL TRIVIA

exoskeleton—the hard covering on the outside of an animal
fluorescent—giving out a bright light by using a certain type of energy; a flourescent light turns light that people cannot see into a light that people can see

Chapter 4
BIZARRE
BEHAVIOR

People can't spit up slime or walk around without heads. But in the animal kingdom, odd behavior is normal. Get ready to meet some animals whose bizarre behavior will leave you scratching your head.

Off with his head!

Hey—not so fast!

A cockroach can still cause some trouble after losing its head. A headless cockroach can walk around for weeks. The cockroach's brain isn't needed for breathing. But without a mouth, it eventually starves to death.

The walnut sphinx caterpillar whistles to scare away hungry birds. But it doesn't use its mouth to squeak. This critter whistles out of holes in the sides of its body. The sound is loud enough for people to hear.

To vomit, some frogs push their stomachs out of their mouths. They wipe their stomachs clean with their front legs. Then they stuff them back inside their bodies.

Humans sweat to cool off. But what if you didn't have any sweat glands? Some vultures and storks have a disgusting way of keeping cool—they pee and poop on their legs. As the liquid in their waste evaporates, it cools the blood.

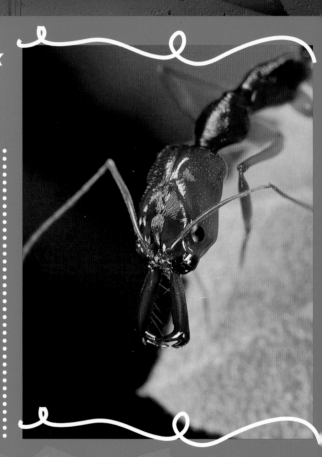

Move over, great white shark. The trap-jaw ant has the fastest bite on Earth. It snaps its jaws shut at up to 145 miles (233 kilometers) per hour. It can chomp down on prey in less than a millisecond.

The pistol shrimp makes a sound like a gunshot by snapping shut its oversized claw. As the claw closes, a jet of bubbles shoots out. The bubbles break and create a shock wave that stuns the pistol shrimp's prey.

Malaysian carpenter ants are walking bombs. The worker ants violently tighten their muscles when threatened. This action causes poison glands inside their bodies to explode. They die protecting the ant colony.

Watch out for flying body parts! When alarmed, some sea cucumbers will blow sticky threads or even internal organs out of their backsides. Startled predators give sea cucumbers time to escape. Sea cucumbers can then regrow these body parts.

Come on, follow me!

Farting in public might seem like bad manners. But herring communicate by passing gas. These fish gulp air and pass it out their backsides to "talk" to one another when it's dark.

Sand tiger sharks are vicious even before they are born. Females carry several pups, but only two are actually born. The developing sharks eat their brothers and sisters until only two remain.

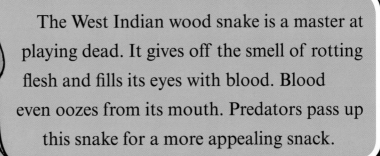

The West Indian wood snake is a master at playing dead. It gives off the smell of rotting flesh and fills its eyes with blood. Blood even oozes from its mouth. Predators pass up this snake for a more appealing snack.

Owls don't make a sound as they swoop toward prey. The feathers on the back ends of their wings reduce noise. Down feathers on the legs and body absorb the rest of the sound. Flight engineers study owl feathers to make quieter airplanes.

SEEING IS BELIEVING

From living in poop to building giant homes, animals amaze us with their unique homes, bodies, and behaviors. When it comes to animal oddities, sometimes you have to see them to believe them!

GLOSSARY

adapt (uh-DAPT)—to change over time in order to survive

evaporate (i-VA-puh-rayt)—to change from a liquid to a gas

exoskeleton—the hard covering on the outside of an animal

fluorescent—giving out a bright light by using a certain type of energy; a flourescent light turns light that people cannot see into a light that people can see

larva (LAR-vuh)—an insect at the stage after an egg

methane (METH-ane)—a colorless, flammable gas produced by the decay of plant and animal matter

microorganism (mye-kro-OR-guh-nis-um)—a living thing too small to be seen without a microscope

nectar (NEK-tur)—a sweet liquid that honey bees gather from flowers

nocturnal (nok-TUR-nuhl)—active at night and resting during the day

nutrient (NOO-tree-uhnt)—a substance needed by a living thing to stay healthy

shock wave (SHOK WAYV)—a burst of quickly moving air

toxin (TOK-sin)—a poisonous substance produced by a living thing

venom (VEN-uhm)—a poisonous liquid produced by some animals

READ MORE

Biskup, Agnieszka. *A Journey into Adaptation with Max Axiom, Super Scientist.* Graphic Science. Mankato, Minn.: Capstone Press, 2007.

National Geographic. *Weird but True! 3: 300 Outrageous Facts.* Washington, D.C.: National Geographic, 2011.

Silverstein, Alvin, Virginia Silverstein, and Laura Silverstein Nunn. *Adaptation.* Science Concepts. Minneapolis: Twenty-First Century Books, 2008.

INTERNET SITES

FactHound offers a safe, fun way to find Internet sites related to this book. All of the sites on FactHound have been researched by our staff.

Here's all you do:

Visit *www.facthound.com*

Type in this code: 9781429676557

Super-cool stuff! Check out projects, games and lots more at **www.capstonekids.com**

INDEX